How Willing Are You?

"Laying a Foundation for Financial Change"

Charmaine Phillips

Table of Contents

Introduction..*vii*
Chapter 1   What Do You Believe?.................11
Chapter 2   Renew Your Mind 19
Chapter 3   Losing Weight 25
Chapter 4   In Debt No More 29
Chapter 5   Broken Vessels 43
Chapter 6   Who Is Walking With You?..........51
Chapter 7   Prepare Yourself 59
Chapter 8   Time To Get To Work...................67
Chapter 9   Living on a Budget......................79
Chapter 10   The Importance of Credit 85
Chapter 11   Vision Planning 95
Chapter 12   Pursuing Your Dreams...............103

Introduction

This book is about my life and my financial experiences. I share some of the accomplishments, mistakes, and lessons I've learned with hopes that it might help you. These events are all steps on a journey I've traveled to achieve financial empowerment and financial freedom. I've found that success is a process of failures, learning, and growing. In your pursuit of success, you'll have to constantly expand your mind and make changes to take you into new areas.

I frequently meet with a group of close friends to review our financial plans. We use that time to give each other feedback on our financial goals, as well as the encouragement to pursue and reach them. In the midst of brainstorming for new ideas, "How Willing Are You?" became a question we kept asking each other. Why, because we had to examine the costs and the necessary changes to bring the goal to reality. We found that we were our greatest obstacles. You have to be willing to sacrifice to achieve the objective. If not — you have failed.

Many people set a goal to become a millionaire. Is that a goal of yours? Are you willing to do what it takes to become wealthy? Why do you want to be wealthy? If you become wealthy, are you going to make an impact in the lives of others, or is it a selfish pursuit? Hopefully, when you look at the basic financial principles and life principles in this book it will change your life!

I hope this book helps you achieve your financial goals. I thank God for allowing me to do this project and pray that it helps you accomplish your financial goals and build generational wealth. I want to speak to you right where you are, whatever level you're on. I want to grab your attention and begin to operate on your life.

I believe this book will change your way of thinking and move you towards financial empowerment, especially because of the use and illustration of biblical principles as a foundation. At times another person's experience can be the best teacher. So digest both my experience and my mistakes as lessons. The information included in this book is from a practical standpoint because to apply some of the lessons would only require simple changes. Are you willing to do it?

If I take something that seems like a Goliath — a giant in your life — and empower you with a practical tip that you can put into place immediately, will you do it so the giant will fall? Some of the paragraphs, or chapters in the book will speak directly to you. When that happens, apply it immediately to your life and make a change. You will see a difference as you renew your mind. You'll start to reprogram your mind, heart and spirit for your benefit.

If you can master the smaller financial precepts, then your financial knowledge and financial strength will consequently grow. If you prove to be unwise in the small financial decisions then you won't be ready for the larger ones. These are principles for good stewards. Why do some people do well financially while others don't? How can another person achieve your goal when you haven't reached it yet? When that happens to me I realize that there's something that I haven't done to get there. When I see that someone did it, it helps me see that I can do the same. It also motivates me to work harder. Don't be discouraged if you are not where you want to be. There are things that you still have to do.

I want to encourage you and I want you to see that change is possible. Don't give up. You will achieve financial freedom that will allow you to pass wealth down to your generations to come.

CHAPTER 1

What Do You Believe?

My pursuit of financial knowledge peaked when I got involved with the finance ministry at my church. Our mission was to teach financial principles from a biblical perspective to as many people as possible. When the people used God's principles in their finances, they started to see positive results and their overall lives improved. Many problems that hinder people are the result of bad financial decisions.

Working in the ministry exposed me to some new financial concepts that impacted me too. Not only did I teach the information to my students, but I applied them to my life. With each class I taught the financial basics to equip the students with the tools to build a strong foundation. Although I had mastered these basics in my personal finances, I finally applied the concepts to my business.

Are you open to learn new financial concepts or do you feel you've already mastered this area? There is always something new that you can use. The world of finance is changing all around us, so an open mind helps you reach new levels. When I surveyed various families on their views on money management, savings, investing, home ownership, and uses of credit cards, their answers varied. Every family operates using different methods to structure their finances. There are various ways to manage money and have a successful result.

The Bible has multiple scriptures on the topic of money because it's essential to our daily lives. In Ecclesiastes 10:19 the Bible says: "A feast is made for laughter, and wine makes merry, but money answers everything." God intends for us to master this area and use the knowledge to gain wealth for His Kingdom. Acquiring wealth is not for our own benefit and level of comfort, but to make an impact in the lives of people that we will come in contact with. For example, in order for the Church to operate in its biblical role in the community and world wide, money is needed to perform ministry. In order to develop programs for people, provide financial assistance in emergency situations, assist families with basic living needs, have food banks, clothing drives and help with housing — money is needed. It takes money to acquire land to build buildings and houses of worship where people can gather. We need money to produce materials that people can learn from, and the list goes on and on.

God built His Kingdom knowing that finances would be an essential element that would make His system operate. He wrote various scriptures addressing the rules of financial money management in order to govern the uses of it and the stewardship of it to benefit His people and the Kingdom as a whole.

Answer these questions for yourself.

How did your financial mind develop? How did you grow up? What did your parents instill in you? What examples did they give you that you practice today? How did they handle money? What were some of their behavior patterns? Did you acquire any financial information from your years in school? Most of the schools you attended probably didn't have formal financial curriculums. Did the topic of money come up in other lessons like in Accounting or Economics? What if there was a formal curriculum that followed you through your education? How would your life be different? What if you were taught financial concepts that were cumulative like in your Math curriculum? What if the financial curriculum was incorporated in the Math curriculum? You learned how to identify, and count coins in Math. Did they teach you how to spend money or were your lessons limited to identifying and counting bills and coins? If you had this in school would you be in a better situation now?

Now consider your environment, or where you grew up. How did this influence you? Do you think there is a big difference from where you grew up and a person who grew up in a neighborhood that was lacking financial resources? Or, if you grew up in the neighborhood with severe lack, do you think the person who grew up in an affluent neighborhood got exposed to different things? Are the makeup or landscape of the buildings different in the two neighborhoods? How would it affect your mind to see a bank replace a check cash store? What if you're used to seeing people drive by in fancy cars versus people standing at the bus stop? What in the environment taught you how people gain wealth? In the neighborhoods, was it very common for you to see people lining up to buy their lottery tickets as a source for them to get wealth?

Was your socioeconomic experience different? Where were your local memberships? Did you get a solicitation to join the professional business clubs where you could meet clients over lunch, or socialize with other business owners? Did you get invited to join the golf or tennis clubs? All these things are like preset channels on a radio that immediately tune you into a certain frequency and prepare you to enter into a world of lack or a world of plenty. How did your parents influence you? It's really amazing when you think about how different life could have been if you were on the opposite side of the long money spectrum. Would you see things differently today? Were you exposed to financial teachings in the Bible? Do you think knowing God's Word had an influence on your financial experience?

These questions should help you to see how your financial mindset was formed. There are business people who don't believe in God, yet follow biblical principles and have successful businesses and generational wealth. The Bible teaches about finances and money. Whether you're saved or unsaved you benefit from applying the Word of God. Once a person accepts Jesus Christ as their personal Savior, they will find that there's another purpose for money. God's plan and purpose for money is different than the world's use of it. The world says to make as much money as you can, spend it, enjoy it, splurge, and satisfy your wants. In God's Kingdom, all the money belongs to Him. It's all His and He expects you to be a steward over it. He asks that you give Him back ten percent (a tithe) of what you have made. This is the income that you earned by using the talents that He gave you. Then He lets you keep the other ninety percent. Although you keep the ninety percent, He is still holding you accountable for what you do with it. That accountability is called stewardship.

In addition to God wanting you to be accountable, he also wants you to be responsible. He's looking to see that you exercise your gifts, talents, and management skills. He wants you to use the ninety percent strategically, not wastefully. God wants to see your faithfulness exercised and then He will delightfully bless you with more. Look at the parable of the talents in Matthew 25:14-30:

(14) "For the kingdom of heaven is like a man traveling to a far country, who called his own servants and delivered his goods to them." (15) "And to one he gave five talents, to another two, and to another one, to each according to his own ability; and immediately

he went on a journey." (16) "Then he who had received the five talents went and traded with them, and made another five talents." (17) "And likewise he who had received two gained two more also." (18) "But he who had received one went and dug in the ground, and hid his lord's money." (19) "After a long time the lord of those servants came and settled accounts with them." (20) "So he who had received five talents came and brought five other talents, saying, 'Lord, you delivered to me five talents; look, I have gained five more talents besides them." (21) "His lord said to him, 'Well done, good and faithful servant; you were faithful over a few things, I will make you ruler over many things. Enter into the joy of your lord." (22) "He also who had received two talents came and said, 'Lord, you delivered to me two talents; look, I have gained two more talents besides them." (23) "His lord said to him, 'Well done, good and faithful servant; you have been faithful over a few things, I will make you ruler over many things. Enter into the joy of your lord." (24) "Then he who had received the one talent came and said, 'Lord, I knew you to be a hard man, reaping where you have not sown, and gathering where you have not scattered seed." (25) "And I was afraid and went and hid your talent in the ground. Look, there you have what is yours." (26) "But his lord answered and said to him, 'You wicked and *lazy servant, you knew that I reap where I have not sown, and gather where I have not scattered seed." (27) "So you ought to have deposited my money with the bankers, and at my coming I would have received back my own with interest." (28) "Therefore take the talent from him, and give it to him who has ten talents."*

He will give you more to steward over when you've shown yourself to be faithful with what you have. It's very different than the world system.

Are you ready to go on this journey and enter into a new dimension? It's time to take your life to another level and submit to the Lord completely. You have to work hard because it's time to bring the vision plan to pass that He's going to accomplish through you. Are you ready to submit your finances to Him? Wouldn't you like to be out of debt? If you get your credit repaired, establish a budget, and faithfully give, you will become financially stronger. Then you would be able to volunteer your time to share your talents to help other people.

COMMITMENTS FOR FINANCIAL CHANGE

- *I am a manager of God's financial resources.*
- *I agree to keep an open mind.*
- *I will live a debt free life.*
- *I will be a charitable giver.*
- *I will build a strong financial foundation in all that I do.*
- *I will constantly pursue financial knowledge.*
- *I will improve my financial vocabulary.*
- *I will be a good steward over my financial resources.*
- *I will keep my word, pay what I owe, and operate in integrity.*
- *I will provide financial knowledge to my children at home.*
- *I understand that I will make financial errors.*
- *I will search the root of my financial influence and destroy negative influences.*
- *I can always learn something new in the area of finances.*
- *I will pursue wealth so that I can influence others.*
- *I will leave a financial legacy that touches four generations.*

CHAPTER 2

Renew Your Mind

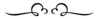

Financial empowerment calls for a change in mindset – a renewed mind. If you examine the way you view your finances, and the methods by which you make decisions like those reviewed in the first chapter, you'll see that the process has to change. We want to be financially free, so we purchase every book on financial freedom looking for that formula to give us the "get rich quick" recipe. If there were a simple formula for gaining wealth, then everyone would be able to do it. But there's no quick and simple way. Why do you think the population of rich people in our country so small?

I'm trying to spread financial information to the masses in the hope that relationships with money will be reevaluated. Just basic fundamental financial education will establish a new understanding about money. You can develop a new understanding of its purpose. You can realize how to get out of debt and maintain a lifestyle that doesn't promote debt. You can learn to live on a budget, and be a good steward over the resources that you have. This places you one step closer in the journey to reach a level of financial empowerment.

Part of the problem, may be that your mindset was formed inaccurately. It's time to go back to the root of these thoughts and actions and destroy them, planting new patterns of thinking instead. Once you reorganize your thought pattern, and subsequently your behavior, then your decision-making process will change. This is important because it's information that you'll pass to the next generation.

What is the specific work that you've been called to do? How are you going to get to that point and how do your finances play a role in propelling you forward? If there is something that you're supposed to do, be determined until you accomplish it. Let God guide you through your challenges. Don't rely on other things. Do you talk yourself out of accomplishing what you need to do? What do you believe? How strong is that belief? What can you do in order to increase your faith? Are you ready to believe what God's Word says for your life? Do you believe the things God spoke to you in your private time? What is discouraging you? How are you going to encourage yourself? By answering these questions you will begin to reprogram your mind.

Strong beliefs can't be shaken, even when you encounter obstacles. One such obstacle can be wrong timing. At a time when things aren't working out like you expect, it's usually because of timing. At a later date, those same issues may resolve themselves. In Ecclesiastes 3:1 the Bible says: "To everything there is a season, a time for every purpose under heaven." Just remember, everything has its time. Just be persistent and review God's principles daily. Stay grounded in His Word so that He can guide you and give you direction. Focus your mind on Him.

I identified that people who don't have a strong foundation are stuck in a mindset of dependency. If you want financial freedom but won't renew your mind then you feel other people are responsible for you. You project your issues on other people because you want someone else to be responsible for the things that you need to do. You approach people in leadership not for support in something you are already doing, but for them to take the responsibility to help more than they should.

This is a prevalent occurrence when it comes to financial help. Financial assistance should be given in difficult times, but it shouldn't be recurring. Renew your mind and know that YOU are responsible for YOU. Now you can focus on God and let Him guide you in the right direction. Your parents may not be there to take care of you, so what you do for you affects you. If your parents weren't there for you in the past, don't use that as an excuse. You can't shift blame to other people. You have to renew your mind and know that whatever your destiny is, you control it. Whoever you want to be is possible. It's up to you to make sure that every need you have is met. If help comes from somewhere else then that's a benefit, but don't rely on it.

It is important for you to know that you are in charge and in control. God trusts you to study His financial principles and apply them. You have to take responsibility for yourself. When you understand this, you will wake up everyday saying, "What do I need to do today to reach my goals?" Align yourself with other people who share similar goals as you and help each other. Sometimes you will position yourself with like-minded people and gain some help in a challenging area. Focus on your source, God, and you will not fall short.

COMMITMENTS FOR FINANCIAL CHANGE

- *I will depend on God as my source.*
- *I am in control.*
- *I am responsible for me.*
- *I will remain encouraged.*
- *I will renew my mind daily.*
- *I will pursue my goals daily.*
- *I will live a modest lifestyle.*
- *I will not be dependent on others.*
- *I will avoid get rich quick schemes.*
- *I will not gamble my financial resources.*

CHAPTER 3

Losing Weight

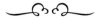

Now that you have a new and renewed mind you will start to see your life through spiritual eyes. With your new vision you will see that there are some areas in your life that need changing. Have you ever set a goal to lose physical weight? Maybe you had a desire to be healthier, look better, and have your clothes fit better. You may have had various reasons, but whatever the motivation, you set a goal to lose weight and shed some of those unwanted pounds.

The process of wanting financial freedom is very similar. There isn't a day that goes by that I don't calculate my debt. Each morning I balance my accounts on my computer against my accounts that I view online. During the evening checks are posted and deposits are credited to my account, so I balance daily. The debt in my life is bondage and a huge weight. It causes a feeling of heaviness. Are you weighted down too? How would you feel if you could shed the weight of the bills and other financial responsibilities?

In weight loss, immediate results can be seen - by simply changing eating habits. Weight programs usually focus on the size of the portions, but a change in the type of foods to more beneficial items like fresh and healthy vegetables, results in greater change. Usually, the root problem is connected to a habit that we have that needs to be broken. Do you have a bad eating habit that needs to be eliminated? If we stop the bad habits then we can bring our body back into good health. In I Corinthians 6:19-20 the Bible says: "Or do you not know that your body is the temple of the Holy Spirit who is in you, whom you have from God and you are not your own? For you were bought at a price; therefore glorify God in your body and in your spirit, which are God's."

We have some bad financial habits that we need to destroy. Is there something you can do to see an immediate result? We have various other habits that are hindering us too. We have spending habits that are causing us to be in a lot of debt and are causing other problems in our lives. Are there some parts of your lifestyle that need to be decreased like the food portions? What types of things are you ingesting during your week? Are you reading financial articles or books on financial freedom? What types of people are you surrounding yourself with and what types of conversations are you engaging in? What types of television programs are you ingesting? Can you change your intake and limit negative influences in your life? If there are some things that are hindering you from achieving financial freedom and hindering your relationship with the Lord, you have to break that habit.

Habit forming can be dangerous when it is not positive. You can develop positive habits, or you can develop negative ones. You need to evaluate your habits and identify which ones need to be changed. If these negative habits are not controlled, they'll destroy your life and you will become completely broken.

COMMITMENTS FOR FINANCIAL CHANGE

- *I will change my habits and behavior.*
- *I will remove negative influences in my life.*
- *I will destroy negative spending habits.*
- *I will limit my intake to positive things.*
- *I will read financial articles and books.*
- *I will engage in more conversations about money.*

CHAPTER 4

In Debt No More!

Look at your debt. Do you understand how you got into your situation? What temptations helped you get out of control? Were you tempted with credit cards? Every time you go in the bank, or a store they have gimmicks to get you to apply for their credit cards. They offer you an introductory rate, or a percentage off your first time purchase, but they make their money back on the interest from your future spending.

One of the ways you are manipulated is in the power and influence of advertising. In Proverbs 23:7 the Bible says: "For as he thinks in his heart, so is he." What you feed into your spirit ends up becoming a part of you. In Proverbs 4:23 the Bible says: "Keep your heart with all diligence for out of it spring the issues of life." It's very important that you limit what you allow yourself to hear, see, who you allow to speak into you, or who you spend your time with. It will become a part of who you are.

This is the power of television. There are a lot of trash television programs. Although you may filter and limit what your children watch, you need to do the same with your programming. Are negative influences making their way into your life through music, movies, and videos? What behavior is produced based on what you watch and hear?

Have you ever tried to get into a certain mindset, but thoughts keep distracting you? How did those thoughts enter your subliminal mind? You can use the techniques of advertising and visual images to your advantage. You can feed your mind with positive visual aids. This is why people post goals and dreams on the walls. Listen to the music that makes you feel good and encourages you. Advertisers manipulate you by exposing you to their product. They bombard you with commercials during your favorite show. Have you ever fell asleep with the television on? What did you dream about? Was your dream similar to what was on the television? Use this to your advantage. Go to sleep with meditative music on. It will change how you wake up the next day. Your subconscious picks up more than your conscious.

Advertisers are aware of the power of their influence. They know that if they bombard you with commercials that you'll eventually purchase their product. Advertising is very expensive, but the rewards are great. The advertiser manipulates you to satisfy their financial goals, pushing you into spending and getting everything now whether your income allows it or not. Advertising can work in conjunction with the stores because the stores make it easy for you to spend by offering you credit – a dangerous offer if misused.

You have to get back to the basics — Needs versus Wants — and identify what those are. Don't buy things and say they are needs if they are wants. Have there been things you didn't want and you bought them anyway? You may have things in your closet with tags on them. Do you have things that you bought on an emotional whim? Have you found that you have so much that you have to give some away? We've become very wasteful and we need to get back to basic stewardship principles. We need to understand that we are stewards (i.e., managers) over what God has given us. This means our money and our time. It's not truly ours, but it's the Lord's.

Some of us have extended ourselves into debt in order to support a lifestyle that's actually higher than where we should be living. Assess your personal situation and identify if this is an issue that needs to be corrected in your life. If so, decide to change that today.

I don't think anybody wants to be in debt. Debt is bondage, slavery, and being obligated to pay another money. If we would use debt appropriately, we could use other people's money to leverage different business ideas or interests that others have and actually gain wealth and benefit from debt. But debt has been misused in our society. Unfortunately society is structured to encourage us to be in debt so that businesses can prosper at our expense. We are encouraged to get credit cards. We're encouraged to buy more than our income, and live above our means. Our society is not going to change how its financial system is structured, so your only recourse is to change so that you're not a part of that world system. In Proverbs 22:7 the Bible says: "The rich rules over the poor and the borrower is servant to the lender." Use this to change your household's management so that your future generations, your children's children, won't be affected by the negative results that so many are experiencing as a result of debt and bondage.

Everyone desires to be debt free, not having to work, or working for pleasure. We work because we have to, because we have obligations — obligations above and beyond our expenses. Most of us are working beyond meeting our basic needs because we have other debt obligations. That's our fault. We can blame society for setting up a system that deceived us, but when you come into revelation knowledge and find truth, that truth should make you free. Sometimes we come to the truth and we reject it. Sometimes God makes it clear to us how things need to be, but we're not willing to change.

Evaluate the debt that you have. Is it good debt or bad debt? For example, my rental properties can be considered good debt because a tenant is paying the mortgage and it creates, or has the potential to create, cash flow when occupied. However, if it is vacant the debt may become a burden. Evaluate your debt and develop a new plan.

Now that you see that there is a change that needs to be made, you need to reprogram your mind, your heart, and your lifestyle, evaluating needs versus wants. You need to look at some root issues and how you got into debt in the first place. I've watched many females ruin their financial situation trying to find a mate. They would charge and spend excessively to maintain and enhance their physical appearances. Their desire was to attract a potential mate, but instead and they found themselves in financial trouble from their personal upkeep and fashion purchases. Their attempts to position themselves socially added up financially.

If you don't spend responsibly you'll wake up one day to maxed out charge cards and the threat of having to file bankruptcy due to out of control spending. Using the illustration of the women above, their root issue was their desire for a mate and it put them in a financial hole. Likewise, you have to look at root issues because when you pray for deliverance from certain things in your life, you can't just deal with the surface. You need to get to the root of the problem and destroy it like pulling weeds in the yard. If you don't get to the root, you're still going to have a problem on the surface. Admit that there is a problem, and decide to change.

Decisions should be followed by practical actions, in this case, a plan. Identify your creditors, and make a list of your debts. You have to know where you are. Repent for those past sins, because you've wasted money in interest and late fees. That's more money that could've gone toward ministry. Debt robs the Kingdom of God of money that could do good work. Ministry needs financing, because blessing and changing the lives of the people of God requires money.

Once you've made the list of your creditors and you've repented for that debt, then you need a plan of action to repay them. Some of the debts on your list are currently on your repayment schedule, but there may be some that are not. Your goal should be to make monthly payment to all your creditors until they are paid off. Develop a plan that would work best for you.

Some techniques include paying off the accounts with the highest interest, or paying off your lowest balances. People always ask me if they should get a consolidation loan. As a rule of thumb, I don't encourage it, because consolidating debt creates larger bills and hinders the process of paying them off. People usually benefit from consolidating if they're going to keep the debt. The consolidation loan makes their debt more manageable. You want to eliminate the debt all together. You don't want to take money from Peter to pay Paul and consolidate Peter and Paul's debt together. You should get rid of it all as quickly as possible. Once you have a plan for paying off debt, then see how long the plan will take. Don't get discouraged if there's a lot that you have to do. In order to pay the debt with your current income, it will require a budget.

Pray this prayer:

"Lord, I was in error. I was living above my means and beyond control. I was out of order. My lust took over. Lord, I am ready to change.

I'm ready to serve You and I need to be free from this bondage. Lord, I need your help. Whatever You tell me to do in order to make this happen, I submit to You. Amen."

Make this confession, make a commitment, and believe it. If you pray this prayer the Lord may tell you to change your lifestyle. You may need to get rid of some of your material things. Are you willing to do that? You may not like what He'll tell you to do. If you are willing, make that confession and wait for His answer. God can do whatever He wants to do. Once you've identified your debt, He can work supernaturally.

One year at my church we believed that in that year we would be debt free. We made a list of all of our debts and we had a debt-burning service. In the spirit realm, the debts were burned, but I knew when I went home my bills would still be on my desk. Before we burned the debt list, I made a copy of it and I posted it where I could see it. I would encourage you to post your debt list, not to discourage you, but to empower you. I remember each time I crossed one of those debts off the list. I crossed them off with a dotted line because I wanted to know that the debt was gone, but I still wanted to see what the debt was. Every time I looked at the list, it didn't discourage me to see how much I owed, but it encouraged me to see how much I no longer owed. I continued to confess. I continued to pray and ask the Lord to show me how the rest of the debt was going to be paid in that year. I knew that normally with the budget that I had it would have taken years in order for that debt to be gone. So God would have to intervene. That year my business increased enough to meet my expenses, pay off all of my debt and establish a reserve account.

You may need an increase to eliminate all of your debt. What can you do to make increase happen in your budget? Can you get a better job? Your life should be a progression so you should strive to go higher. As you do, your debt will be reduced because your income is a major source of paying bills. You can be content with your job because it's for a season, but always push higher because you have to reach your destiny. You can be financially free and financially independent and you can have a stream of wealth.

When you have debt, you don't have the luxury of being content because you have to push higher and increase your income stream. Once you eliminate your debt, you don't have to push anymore. You can go back to being content and working just enough hours to meet your living expenses, and adding a little extra for reserves. As long as you have outstanding debt it's robbing the Kingdom of God of money, so you must press to change that situation. Don't be content. You don't have to live a life in debt. Reach for higher opportunities. As you obtain increase, you will accomplish both goals: eliminating debt and moving forward with the vision plan for your life.

God is trying to turn you away from debt. He renews your mind and changes your old ways. Debt can be like a bad relationship. Debt puts such a veil or spirit over you so that it controls your daily life. It keeps you under control and in bondage. It robs your freedom, and hinders you from serving God. The Bible says in Romans 13:8 to "Owe no one anything except to love one another, for he who loves another has fulfilled the law." The only person that you should owe anything to is Christ. You owe Him thanksgiving, and praise. Our world system has caused confusion and mislead us. It makes us put so much before God. When you are in debt, so much has to be paid or responded to before you can respond to the Lord. Nothing should have that kind of control over you, or your relationship with Christ.

Many foreign countries are run on a cash and carry basis. They appear to have less than we do because they don't have a credit system. They can't purchase a vehicle or a home unless they have saved enough cash. They work hard, save for years, and then get the things they want. Many foreigners come to this country with large amounts of cash, but have very little material possessions. They understand that they have to sacrifice and save for the big purchases. It's going to take commitment, time, and possibly several family members, immediate and extended, pulling together to make that dream a reality.

We lose our ability to work toward our goals because credit has made it easy to have those things without having to wait. This changes us because nothing in our lives is appreciated any more. We want instant gratification and rewards now. In every aspect of our lives, we expect to see things come very quickly. That has caused us to bypass process and it has caused us to bypass some of those things that God meant for us to have to go through. Process helps us when we get to another level. We gain knowledge and maturity from the process. Our world system has allowed us to skip several steps, and those bad habits are crossing over into other aspects of our lives and relationships. Debt and credit has a much more powerful impact on us than we may realize. It is important for you to be free to worship, free to serve, free to give your time, and give offering.

In order to get out of debt, you have to stop spending. You have to evaluate your use of credit cards. You have to evaluate how many of them you have and why. You may have a lot of duplicate cards that you don't need. So you want to look at the credit cards you have, why you have them, and why you have the amount that you have. Close the accounts that you don't need. You have to do some things to discipline yourself. If you don't have ten cards anymore, then you won't use ten cards to their maximum limit. So, start to change some of these things.

Once you look at the credit that you have, close some accounts and put yourself on a spending freeze. Add up the debt. Every month, after you pay your expenses, eliminate a debt by applying your excess money toward it. Once you make a commitment to be debt free things may get tight. It will be better to make these changes now, than to continue paying interest, late fees, and other charges on previous purchases. Each time a debt is paid, your income will start to go further.

Your plan should be to renew your mind, operate in something that you're passionate about, and master the different stages and levels of work. Once you have the money you'll know what to do with it. Now budget that money so that you can use it to achieve other goals. Once you eliminate your debt, don't go in the wrong direction again. Avoid the pitfalls of debt in your individual life or with your businesses.

Income, budgeting and debt, are three areas in your life that you have to control. As you learn this financial information immediately apply it to your household. Financial behavior changes can occur in a short period of time. If you review the number of credit cards you have and eliminate some because of duplication that's an example of immediate change. Many people keep a lot of cards in case something happens but when you track your spending you realize most of your spending was things that you didn't have to spend on, not emergencies. Close these accounts because they just get you in trouble when the advertisers decide to manipulate you for their marketing purposes.

How do you feel when your children are influenced in how they dress, the words they say, or the music that they listen to? It's frustrating when you see them succumb to peer pressure, drink, do drugs, or engage in some activity that goes against their moral beliefs. Are you doing the same thing? Your peers influence you with their cars, their employment status and their homes. Most of it is a facade because they don't own those assets and their status is not based on true wealth. A lot of people drive cars they don't own, but lease. Or some of the people that you envy pay huge amounts of money for that lifestyle.

Stop trying to compete with them. Their lifestyle may not be what it seems.

We make purchases with cash or cash equivalents. What if you could get some things without needing cash? You have overflow or abundance in your households, meaning that if you examine your household, you have things that you don't need. Maybe you needed them at some point, but you don't need them anymore. Someone you know needs that very thing that you don't use anymore. What if you traded your abundance with them for something you need? This is a barter system.

In a no cash system, you find people to trade goods or services with, to eliminate the need for cash. You can find several friends and start a barter group. If you decide to form a no-cash type system, the more people in the group the wider variety of things to trade. In any group of twenty to twenty five people of varied ages and varied situations, there are enough resources to meet all needs. Your budget benefits because, cash doesn't go out, and you received things you needed that you would normally have to pay for. The members of the group have to donate their extra time to take care of someone's need. There are things that you are going to do for yourself. There are things that you are going to do with others. The collaboration will push each of you to another level and empower you. If you have the desire but don't know how to do it, you can work with others who also have a need that they can't fit in the budget, and then you can exchange services with each other.

COMMITMENTS FOR FINANCIAL CHANGE

- *I will not be in bondage to debt anymore.*
- *I will make purchases according to my income.*
- *I will not make emotional purchases.*
- *I will avoid temptations.*
- *I will eliminate negative influences.*
- *I will identify my root issues and resolve them.*
- *I will develop a plan and stick to it.*
- *I will not let debt control me.*
- *I will exchange services with others.*
- *I will use short- term debt as leverage for growing a business.*

CHAPTER 5

Broken Vessels

Have you ever been broken? You can go through different trials in your life and sometimes you can be broken as a result of those events. Sometimes God is trying to do something in your life. Sometimes the events are just part of life. You'll live through them, grow from them, mature and realize that things just happen. It could be that a family member has died, a relationship has ended, or a season has changed. You begin to adapt as a result of it and move on.

As you experience periods of brokenness it's important to evaluate your attitude and how you handle that time. You will be a living example to those around you, especially when they know you're a Christian and watch how you handle these situations. Don't allow those situations to break you in such a way that you promote or breed negativity that other people will see. They will mimic your behavior when a similar situation comes along in their life. If somebody is watching you go through a hard time financially and you maintain a level head, when a similar situation happens to them, they would probably do the same.

Sometimes God is trying to do something in your life just for a season. That season may last for a while until He is ready to release you from it. Sometimes a change in your financial situation will remove you from your state of brokenness. You should accept the change, understanding that there is a greater plan ahead. This is why you're going through this season.

Prayer is the first step. Accept responsibility for financial errors that you have made so your situation can change. Look back at your actions and evaluate what you did to get in your situation. You don't want to get released from the season, only to return to it. You want to make sure that when you exit that it is permanent. Identify the behavior that caused your financial predicament. What was your motivation for that behavior and identify the root issue that caused it? Once you have these answers, correct your behavior and change.

You can control the part that you're responsible for. Sometimes, there are situations that are beyond your control. When you find yourself in a situation that you cannot change, change your perspective. Change how you look at it and react to it. Change how it makes you feel. Don't get frustrated or depressed because you can't change the situation. Be at peace about things you cannot control.

How do you handle life when you're just at your lowest? What do you do when you have no money and you are at your lowest? You have to guard against humiliation. Don't be embarrassed. You can control how others will see you by changing how you view your situation. When financial challenges begin, you may have to wear clothes that may not look as good as what you used to wear. How are you going to handle that? Are you going to walk around feeling humiliated because of what you have to wear? Your situation is temporary, so find the laughter in it.

Don't be so embarrassed that you don't ask for assistance. When you try your best, and you've reached your limit, seek help. Someone else may control your exit plan for getting out of that situation. That door may close if you are not willing to receive help. Those feelings of embarrassment can keep you from being delivered.

Sometimes, you have to deal with your emotions and how you perceive a situation. You may be hindering yourself from your release because of pride and ego. Are you concerned about what others are going to think about you? This is why a lot of people get into financial trouble. They're so concerned about their image that they can't improve their financial situation.

You may need to make a radical change in your life. This could include moving back to a parent or guardian's house. If you give up your apartment and move home, will this help you get your finances in order? Of course, you may not want to do that. If your relationship with your family is strained, then look at a roommate situation. Maybe you need to move in with someone in a similar situation like yours. They may have an additional bedroom that you can rent and that arrangement can help you both. You can combine resources together and help each other. For example, if they rent you a room then they have additional money coming in per month for the room that you are renting and your rental expenses has decreased from full rent to a room rate. Be creative and think of other options that could change your situation.

How willing are you? How willing are you to change your situation? I had a person come and ask if they could stay with me for a while and without praying I said yes. I made a huge mistake. I tried to offer her work. I told her that I pay a person to clean my properties, a landscaper to cut my yards, and an assistant to work at my real estate office. I explained to her the different types of work that I had that were opportunities for her make some money. It didn't take long to realize that she really didn't want to work, but preferred to stay in my home for free. She wasn't willing to change. Finally I asked her, "How willing are you?" She immediately responded by saying, "What, to help you?" My answer was, "No. To help you!"

People may think you're trying to exploit them instead of trying to help them. If you don't get this lesson then your situation isn't going to change. You can't feel that it's someone's responsibility to provide you housing or to support you. Try to have the right attitude if you end up in this situation.

Sometimes you receive valuable training when you walk with someone else for a season. When you help them to accomplish their vision it helps you later in your career. The time with them teaches you and prepares you so that when you're ready to go out on your own you have their experience to learn from. You would've seen how they handled good and bad situations.

Do you want to change? Do you need to change? Do you want your descendants to go further than you did? If you start to make changes now and don't see immediate results in your life, then rest assured that it will make a difference in the lives of your children and their children. You'll be the forerunner in your family and set a new standard. You'll be the one that will make sure that they're not going to have to go through what you're going through now. Are you willing to embrace this message?

How willing are you? Are you going to do whatever it takes? When you tell the Lord that you're ready, things are going to start changing for you. This means radical changes may need to take place in your life, your attitude, your work ethic, and your daily schedule. Are you willing to work a double shift? Are you willing to work a part-time job in addition to your full time job? Are you willing to work and go to school at night? These scenarios may solve your financial problems.

At some point you have to realize that the only way things are going to change is if your situation changes. Your daily schedule may have to change. Your television time may decrease, while your reading time increases. You will need to increase your worship and study time with the Lord. You need to make time to fellowship with your brothers and sisters in Christ more. You have to surround yourself with people who are visionaries like you and meet with them often for support. This allows you to feed off of each other and you're able to bless each other by sharing information and encouraging each other.

You have to be willing to do the work and it's not going to be easy. You can't expect that it's going to happen overnight because you didn't get in your situation overnight. You can't expect to come out of your situation instantly because if you were delivered quickly you'd probably go back to it just as fast. If you were delivered quickly, there wouldn't be a level of appreciation for where you are and what you've accomplished. So, deliverance may seem slow because the Lord wants you to remember how uncomfortable you were, how ugly your situation was, and how much you desired to change. When you finally come out of it there is such a bad memory for that part of your life that you don't want to revisit it. You will be in "process." There are different stages, and different steps of process.

How willing are you? Are you willing to sell your home? Many people have equity in their homes but are constantly behind on payments and struggle to maintain it. They focus on the embarrassment of the neighbors seeing them lose it, so they try to hold on to it and ultimately lose both their house and the equity. A house is an asset that can be sold. When you hold on to it too long, the mortgage company begins the foreclosure process. You must evaluate when the situation isn't improving and make adjustments before it's too late.

If you sell your home, the loan payoff will include the payments that you are behind and the loan balance. If things work out you may still have something left over to use for moving expenses or to settle somewhere else temporarily. After getting back on your feet, you can pursue home ownership again at a later date. Don't make the same mistake as the people I've seen who didn't take advantage of the opportunity to sell their home and resettle somewhere more manageable until their situation changed.

COMMITMENTS FOR FINANCIAL CHANGE

- *I won't worry about what I can't control.*
- *My challenges are temporary.*
- *If I'm in trouble I will ask for help.*
- *I am willing to sacrifice to advance myself.*
- *I will learn from my mistakes.*
- *I am willing to change to help my situation.*
- *I will constantly improve myself.*

CHAPTER 6

Who Is Walking With You?

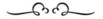

Once you start your rebuilding process and start operating in your new mindset you will need people to support you. Develop a support system of people who will support your vision and give you wise counsel. In Proverbs 19:20 the Bible says: "Listen to counsel and receive instruction, that you may be wise in your latter days." In Proverbs 15:22 the Bible says: "Without counsel, plans go awry, but in the multitude of counselors they are established." These are very important scriptures regarding counseling. Once you select these people, allow them to support you, but make sure you stay in control. If you allow people to control your behavior, they will control your destiny. How many times have you felt like pursuing something and you consulted someone else for approval? It's important to seek counsel from others for wisdom, but not for approval. If you rely on the approval of others it will stifle your growth.

Also you need people to hold you accountable and give you feedback on your plans. Their feedback shouldn't prevent you from moving forward with things you need to do.

You need to look at who your friends are and identify the purpose for your friendship with them. A good friendship provides companionship, support, and wise counsel. Good friends make you better, and help you even when you have different visions. There is a reason that the Lord establishes your covenant relationship with another person. He has a task for the two of you to accomplish collectively. It's why the Lord allowed your paths to cross. Once you develop the relationship it will become rich and deep. You will know how important it is that you walk together.

Evaluate your friendships. Do they fit the description of a covenant relationship, or are they people you only eat with and hang out with? What is it that cannot be accomplished for the Kingdom if the two of you aren't walking together? Is the Kingdom better that the two of you have united? What is the task that you must accomplish together? How is their life going to be different as a result of you being in it and how will yours be different?

We have some friendships that are God-ordained relationships. Some are long term and others are just for a season. If you had a friend who supported you through your education, and after you graduated you realized that you wouldn't have made it through that time period without them and their support, then it probably was a God-ordained relationship. If a person is removed from your life and it has no impact then that was a casual relationship.

Another example could be someone who was a surrogate parent for you when your parent wasn't around. God allowed this person to be in your life during your formative years and they were able to guide, encourage, and support you. Once you grew up their job was completed.

If you have a support group then evaluate the people in it. Are they walking with you pushing you toward your destiny? Selecting the people who will be around you must be a part of your business plan. Anything that you accomplish for God won't be easy and will require more than your gifts and talents. If it is a big vision from God you can't accomplish the task by yourself. There are some things that you can do by yourself, but when you're going to another level some things have to be done with the help of others.

Establish a standard for the people in your circle. You have to evaluate their integrity, and character. Do not surround yourself with people who lack integrity. If they lack honesty and integrity they aren't the people that God wants to walk with you. You cannot build relationships with people who lack honesty. Honest people tell you the truth. The truth can hurt. You may not like what they say, but you will recover from it.

Look at a person's character. How do they operate? How do they treat others in their life? Look at how they deal with issues in their personal life. This gives you an idea of how they're going to conduct business.

Keep that in mind when you invite people into your circle. Who are the people in your life that support your vision and continually keep you accountable? How often do you talk with them? How often do you meet? How often do you give them updates on what you have accomplished and what you're working on? What type of feedback are they giving you to ensure that you have fulfilled your objectives? Do they give you positive feedback and constructive criticism? Is their feedback given in a manner that encourages you and lifts you, or does it make you feel worse? Are you of like mind and spirit? Are you on one accord? Are you equally yoked in abilities and spiritually with your business partners? Is this a positive person who is speaking the same language as you? If not, it could be a hindrance to your progress. Evaluate these relationships carefully.

If you have the same mindset as your circle of friends, they will encourage you in the hard times and remind you that you can accomplish whatever you set your mind to. With these forms of support your foundation is strengthened. Look at the people in your circle and make sure they are giving you the support that you need to accomplish your vision. Look for people who have similar visions because as you're walking that path, you are walking it together. The two of you should be sharpening each other and moving each other forward. In Proverbs 27:17 the Bible says: "As iron sharpens iron, so a man sharpens the countenance of his friend." One person may be gathering information in a particular area that's complimenting what you're working on.

They can share that information with you and save you from researching that information. Now you can move forward on your plan. You want to look at the people in your circle and make sure you're surrounding yourself with people who share your vision or people who love you and want to see what you're doing come to pass.

How helpful or detrimental is your family right now to your goal? Do they ridicule you? Do they give you support or are they speaking against everything that you come up with? If you study the story of Abraham in the bible, the Lord had to tell Abraham to get away from his relatives in order to accomplish what he needed through him. In the life of Joseph, his brothers threw him in a pit to die. At that time his family was not operating in his best interest. But God is so awesome. He used that situation and worked it out for His good. Joseph was able to continue on the path that God ordained for him. He didn't die as they had planned because God stepped in to rescue him, and to use Joseph for His purpose. God elevated him, blessed him, and Joseph was able to go back and save his bloodline in spite of what they did to him.

Evaluate your family. You want to keep a relationship with them, but sometimes you have to disconnect from them in order for you to focus and accomplish what God is saying to you.

Early on in my life, I knew the Lord was telling me to acquire real estate. A relative — with all good intentions — told me not to buy a home because she felt it would cause unnecessary stress. She advised me to get an apartment, save my money and then go from there. I didn't feel that was God's plan so I went ahead and bought a piece of property. I don't regret that decision and I have bought many properties since then. I believe that if I had listened to her and just rented, then I wouldn't be the person that I am today and I wouldn't have my current real estate portfolio.

Sometimes with good intentions and love, your family is going to speak against the things God is telling you to do and the things that need to be accomplished through you for the Kingdom. Do you need to remove yourself and get away from them? You have to be careful to receive counsel from family if it lines up with what God has already given you instruction about. Do not listen to people who speak contrary to what the Lord has told you.

Your family can also hinder you by constantly asking for your financial support. They may drain you and put you into a financial bind if they haven't handled their finances properly and they've mismanaged their funds.

For example, if you have a relative who is about to get evicted, you should only help to the extent that you are able. Sometimes people need to hit rock bottom in order to see and know that the hand of God is on their lives.

We hinder God from blessing our family or from coming to their rescue because we become God to them. For some of the people in your family, you are God. You are their salvation. When family members get in trouble they don't call on God, they call you. You perpetuate the cycle because when they call on you, you answer, and when they say they need, you give. Sometimes you feel good about always being the one that rescues them. Sometimes the support you gave them was contrary to God's plan for their life.

Some support that you give can be excessive. When people need you to bail them out of a situation but they haven't changed the thing that got them into that situation, you'll find that they will be back in that same situation very soon. They will look for you to bail them out once again. You have to stop supporting others in order to get your own financial picture in order. It means saying no to their requests. Sometimes this will offend them, but I believe if you say no it will cause change in their lives. You want them to get delivered, move forward, and fish for themselves.

COMMITMENTS FOR FINANCIAL CHANGE

- *I will develop a support group.*
- *I will not provide or receive unhealthy support.*
- *I will walk with people of like mind and spirit.*
- *I will evaluate the purpose of my relationships.*
- *I will evaluate my family's role in my calling.*
- *I will seek wise counsel.*

CHAPTER 7

Prepare Yourself

You'll experience some challenging situations in your life, but they'll help you grow. Things aren't going to be easy. You'll have some challenges and you need to prepare for them. This is all a part of your life cycle. When things are going well, be like the animals that store up for the Winter. When you have those Winter seasons or tough times, you would've prepared for it. You need a cushion for your needs. When things are good, most people live at the highest standard they can but don't prepare for the rainy days.

You have to take the Word that God spoke to you and evaluate the time frame it will take to manifest itself. Your plans will not manifest overnight. We have to balance our spirituality with practicality. For example, if we were talking about healing, God can heal my body immediately. In the same moment that I believe my body can be healed, He can heal me.

However there are things that God is requiring of you to change your situation. He says He will make a way and be your provider to sustain you and to build your vision. He does this because it is His vision for your life that He gave you. There are some things He needs you to do to go ahead and progress in His plan. He is already pouring out blessings, but are you in position to receive them? God is saying that most of this requires your participation. He says that He is already involved in your process. This is because from the beginning of time He already ordained the path for you to travel. He needs you to connect to Him, hear Him, understand Him, and believe in Him. Believe in the Christ in you that these things might manifest. Your success requires your belief, and commitment. Surround yourself with people who echo what God said, and support what you are called to accomplish.

God needs you to go and do some things. Go and apply for permits. Go get your license. Complete your education. Write the vision. Write some letters and make contact with some people. Call some people who are going to help you move your vision plan forward. Hire some professionals that are going to assist you with those things that will fall outside of the area of your expertise. Do some things to help your situation. He has already paved the way and lined up the people. All you have to do is walk in it.

So many of us have failed to just walk in what He's already given us. We're not catching the blessings He's already pouring out. We're not reaching up and grabbing the things that are already there in the realm that we're in. We're not stepping into another dimension where things are. We still want to operate on a lower level. God is putting the responsibility back on us to go ahead and get what He's already promised us. If you are not there, it might be your fault.

Timing is so important because you have to first discern what your role is. You have to determine the time frame in which you are to execute your particular responsibilities so that everything will line up and come together as it has been ordained. Start looking at time frames and things that need to occur in the natural. If the Lord is telling you about a business or franchise, then you should have already contacted that franchise business to get the information on the cost. These are levels of preparation that require your participation so things can happen.

Do a self- assessment and then decide what you want to do. In order for you to obtain and be successful at certain jobs, you have to meet the qualifications and obtain the skills that meet the requirements for the position. This will begin with the educational component that will provide a proper foundation. Sometime this will require finances and that may pose a challenge. You may have to find a way to educate yourself through alternative means. Research the field that you want to be in by reading books and training manuals on the topic.

Try to find an apprenticeship under someone who is doing exactly what you want to do. Follow them around and get training as you work. Formal higher education may not be available for everyone. If you don't do the formal training or the alternative you won't have the skills or the experience to qualify for certain types of jobs.

Are you willing to work for someone without pay? This could be an opportunity for you to learn from their experiences and wisdom. Do you see the value in working just to acquire information? Do you see value in learning without receiving a paycheck? We work to take care of our financial needs, so we do have a need to receive a paycheck. But if you misuse your check and operate without a budget, then you won't meet your needs. Is your ultimate goal to progress? Is your ultimate goal to change? Are you happy with just getting by? Are you content with living from paycheck to paycheck? Do you want to just meet your needs and not go any further?

If your goal is to progress, then spend two hours in an apprentice or intern position after you get off of your regular job. You don't see many people applying for internships because people don't want to do something unless they're getting something. We have to nurture the mentality that self-improvement can be more valuable than compensation.

Do you want to stay in your current job and remain miserable, or do you want to sacrifice, intern, gain the knowledge, and be able to leave? You need to seek the knowledge that's going to get you into the field that you want — your passion. Your wealth will be generated when you're doing the thing that you want to do. It will be a pleasure to go to work, because you are operating in your destiny. It won't feel like work because you'll be operating in who you are. It will be better than you could imagine. So make sacrifices for yourself.

We are conditioned to believe that anybody who suggests that we work for them for free is trying to take advantage of us. That mentality hinders your progress, because what you get is professional improvement. The knowledge you gain will ensure a permanent income stream in years to come.

If you find someone to mentor you, then know that it cost them to take time to give you instruction and guidance. If the mentor can earn $100 per hour in their profession, and they spend one hour mentoring you, it costs them $100 in potential lost revenue. They could be somewhere else talking to someone and generating money. They have lost that opportunity because they took the time to help develop you. Don't think the time you spend with them is without financial compensation. Look at it from a different perspective. The world teaches us that everybody should focus on what they can get. It teaches you to ask, "What can you do for me? What am I going to get?"

What you're going to receive is the knowledge and information that you need to be independent — to stand on your own, and to be successful. After that you will be able to give back to someone else. So many professionals will give that hour to help someone else because we probably received the same when we were trying to elevate ourselves. Personally it's worth it to sacrifice what I can be doing in that hour, so that a person can go forward and be successful too. How willing are you?

If you had a mentor when you were young, they would have provided guidance to help you decide your career path. You made a career decision based on what you were exposed to and the limited knowledge you had. Your career might be different if you were exposed to more choices early in life.

COMMITMENTS FOR FINANCIAL CHANGE

- *I will plan my life goals.*
- *I will discern the season I am in.*
- *I will get the credentials I need to reach my goals.*
- *I will study to gain knowledge.*
- *I will prepare for times of famine.*
- *I will sacrifice for my dreams.*

CHAPTER 8

Time To Get To Work!

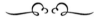

I grew up in a big city and I started working early. I worked during the summer through the city youth program. When I attended high school, I worked after school in a co-op job. My high school was a specialized school and was geared toward business careers. Through the co-op program I was placed in a job on Wall Street. I always had a business mindset, but my high school helped to develop it more. The job exposed me to business etiquette and broadened my business knowledge. I gained a real good work ethic early. In some of my job experiences I would work from the time I got up until it was time to rest. This prepared me for my adult schedule where I juggle several jobs and manage multiple streams of income.

A good work ethic begins during childhood. Children are taught work ethics through chores and household responsibilities. This establishes a strong work foundation. These early responsibilities help a child become a better adult and forms invaluable character. Without this foundation an excellent work ethic may prove to be quite challenging.

A good work ethic is also formed if a person is taught stewardship principles. If a parent buys a child toys and the child doesn't take care of them, poor stewardship is taught if the parent replaces the damaged and misused toys. Children need to learn to take care of the things that are given to them. This includes the stewardship of their time and resources. These lessons translate to adult behaviors in the workplace.

When you were young, did anyone assign you a responsibility that held you accountable? Did you have a job like cutting grass or washing cars? Did you exercise faithfulness, and give each assignment your best? Did you have pride in the work that you did? What was your attitude? Some of the experiences you had in your youth have led to your work ethic as an adult.

The world's standard puts such a priority on making money that we loose the desire to learn and gain knowledge. I always said a college education is free because I attended a large university. Some of the classes I attended were in large auditoriums with so many people that no one knew if I was there or not. They never took attendance and my school was in an environment where if you missed class, it went unnoticed. You had to be mature enough and disciplined enough to do what you were supposed to do. If anyone entered the campus, got a schedule and some books from the bookstore, they could go to class for free and no one would ever know. Schools don't worry about anyone doing that because most of us go to college for credentials. We pursue higher education for a degree. We need the degree to give us validation that there are certain things that we know so that an employer would hire us and be comfortable with paying us a wage level that we feel good about. We want a record that we were there.

Unfortunately we've created a society where nobody pursues education for the knowledge. I believe that most of us were taught that you go to college to get a job, and a small group of us were taught that you go to college to gain knowledge. Some mention that college is a good place to meet people from different places and get an experience that you can treasure for a lifetime. These experiences help make up a good portion of who you are going to become. We should've been taught that we could become the people who could create jobs and businesses or be entrepreneurs. Instead we were conditioned to continue the same cycle of our parents where we work for money and never learned how to make money work for us.

Many graduating students from college expect the best jobs immediately. They have no experience yet believe they're entitled to high-paying jobs without starting at the ground floor level. You don't have to enter at the very bottom, but an entry-level position with a great employer will provide good experience, and knowledge in the field. You may feel that your position is not providing the knowledge that you want, but you can learn from any job even if it's temporary and not in your field. We all need to make a living and need to work, so use the time that you are working for someone else to support your livelihood and provide opportunities to learn.

There are some basic principals related to work. You need a job or income to support yourself. In 2 Thessalonians 3:10 the Bible says: "For even when we were with you we command you this, if anyone will not work neither shall he eat." It was God's intention for man to work. God uses work to meet your needs as He moves you into your destiny. Adam got his first job in the garden.

When you become an adult you find a job that suits you. With the income that you earn you meet your needs and wants. Your income size needs to be large enough to accommodate your family size and needs. Are you someone who gets up in the morning ready to work, or does someone have to push you to do eight hours? Income and our ability to earn it is one of the reasons we have problems today with financial success or financial freedom.

Do you know people who feel others are responsible for supporting their basic needs? These people solicit their family members and friends, and other charitable people, for handouts. Their root problem might be laziness, or unbelief. They don't believe that they have the ability to do it, so they depend on others. Their root problem could be lack of self-esteem, lack of education, or inadequacy. They can't be successful until they overcome these issues. There are times that people suddenly become unemployed.

Some had great office jobs and suddenly don't have an income. They are too proud or prideful to take certain types of jobs. They feel it is beneath them or embarrassing for other people to see them in other positions. Also, they are unable to maintain the lifestyle that they were accustomed to and don't want to shift to something temporarily. So it is necessary for you to know how to find work, seek work, and keep work! You need income because you can't expect other people to support you. If you are able, then you should be working.

If you focus on the importance of working you will keep other problems from happening that are related to financial lack. Many people lose their homes, cars, other assets, relationships, marriages, and hinder family relationships by mismanaging their finances. They borrow too much money, spend excessively or disproportionate to their income, and accumulate unnecessary debt. Then they want the church, family and friends to provide them money to help them pay rent or feed their children. Help should be there for you if you have done everything you can and still don't have enough, but not when you mismanage what should cover your needs. People mismanage their resources and then guilt you into feeling you should do for them. Watch out for these spirits that people inflict on you. When you help someone it should be out of overflow and not out of requirement or guilt. You can hinder other people in moving forward in what God has for them when they become dependent on you. Many people earn sufficient income but don't live on a budget. This causes them to have problems managing their spending, and debt.

If managing your resources is not something that you have accomplished yet, then you need to make some changes. You control your destiny. I know God will reveal to you where you need to be. When he does, just do it.

Pray this prayer:

"Lord I thank you for the help I received from others in the past, but I believe that you intend for me to meet all of my needs relying on you completely. Please direct my path. Reveal to me the things that I need to do to improve my situation. Help me have a willing heart to do them. Lord put me in a position that I don't need financial help from others, but actually become someone who can help others in their time of need. Amen."

Unless you have sufficient money to support yourself, then working is not an option at this time. Your first job doesn't have to be your perfect dream job. It's simply a vessel of support. It may not be the job that God has called you to be in. It's probably not in your field of choice.

Even though you may know it's temporary, work for a reasonable amount of time with the employer so that when another opportunity comes along your exit isn't abrupt. You should always be professional in taking a job. When you accept a job, give them a reasonable commitment, and continue looking while you are working.

Now at different stages of your life you will earn income in jobs where your function is not that thing that you love to do. These types of jobs are for a season and aren't your destiny position. For example, a student may work a part time position that helps earn money for books. You may work a job during the Christmas season so that you will have money for gifts. Another example could be an intern-ship that is used to gain experience. Understand and know that these different positions that you hold are temporary and they will springboard you to that place you desire to be. Don't get stuck in the job that, "I don't want to be in, but it pays the bills right now." Realize your current situation is not the end. There's something else that you are striving for and you will get there through a progression of different stages of work. Break out of your pattern of getting up every day to work, pay the bills, and repeat the cycle the next day.

You need to embrace the different seasons in your life. There are going to be different rings of the ladder that you'll have to climb and each job that you have will prepare you for something greater. You should enjoy the season that you are in and learn from it because God is going to use it to take you somewhere else. Continue to let God show you things in this time. Learn from Him and then get prepared because when the season changes you need to be ready to move with Him.

There are seasons in which you will serve others and help bring their visions to pass. In that season celebrate their success knowing that your time will come also. Sometimes your success comes through assisting someone else. You may not be the visionary or the person up front. Many people think that only up front and visible people are successful, but you can be a huge success, and reach you goals from behind the scenes.

Whatever gifts God has placed in you; He expects you to utilize them. The person who will be out front will get ridiculed and may suffer many challenges because they'll bear most of the responsibilities. If your role is to help, then your role is just as important, and probably part of your preparation for where God is taking you. Be faithful in that time of service because whether it's a paid position or an internship, it's a season of preparation.

You will have several jobs before you get into your career. You will find your career when you become passionate about your work. It will be something that you're good at, and skilled at. When you work in your gift, you can work fourteen hours a day and it won't feel like it, because you love what you do. This will be the job that you'll stay with, build on and generate the largest amount of income. This is when you'll be moving toward your destiny.

As you exercise faithfulness in your work, there are lessons that you can learn. You must be open to hear from God and continue to faithfully serve no matter what position you are in. Do you know people who steal from the person or company that they work for? It's ironic, but the same people who steal want to start their own business. There's a direct correlation between your faithfulness on your job and your success in running your own business. In Luke 16:10 the Bible says: "He who is faithful over another man's shall get his own." In Luke 16:12 the Bible says: "He who is faithful over the little shall be rulers over much."

More people put Luke 16:12 to practical application while ignoring Luke 16:10. But when you're on a job and you're not faithful over that man's business, you cannot expect the Lord to bless you with your own business. This means you haven't mastered the relationship between your stewardship over someone else's and your request of God to bless you with your own.

Many employees exercise poor stewardship. For example, they recognize that stealing money from the employer is wrong, but how they use your time on the job could be considered stealing. If you're conducting a lot of personal phone calls while on the job, that's a form of stealing. You're stealing the time that you're being paid for to do a function that you're not doing. You may not steal time or supplies from your employer, but what do you do when there's a lot of dead time? Do you make some personal phone calls, or read a book? Good stewardship means you do something to help the business go forward. You should also utilize the time that you're being paid to make something happen that is not happening now. Take some initiative and prepare for something that will be needed next week. These are behavior patterns that if not exercised now will make you deficient on the next level. If you want a promotion from God, you have to be faithful in what you're already doing. This is your training for a higher position or to start your own business.

We are all striving for financial freedom, and working is a big part of achieving it. If you have a vision to start a business, don't quit your job in order to start the business. This is one of the biggest mistakes that people make. They get excited, have received a vision for a business, and immediately leave their job. As an employee, your purpose is to get information and experience so that when you start your own business you'll understand all aspects of the field. When you become an employer or small business owner you will have a different perspective.

The transition should not only include your new business matching your full time income but should also include a large reserve account. If not, you will find yourself further behind from getting the business started because your personal household is lacking due to insufficient income. If you want to ensure your success, start your business as a side job, as a part-time supplement to your full-time job. Continue to be faithful on your regular job and build your business during your breaks, and after work. Once your business is producing sufficient income in order to support you as your primary job does, then you can resign.

When you're ready to launch out on your own, find something that you love to do. Create a business opportunity with the thing that you are passionate about. Hire employees that share your vision. This helps you to leverage your time. They will support and help you accomplish more for your business. You should still maintain a strong work ethic even when you have others helping you.

When you work and receive a paycheck that is a one to one relationship. If you don't work, you won't get paid. Overtime, part-time jobs, and double shifts are good for short-term financial goals, but you can't physically do the hours that it would take to gain wealth. Wealth is generated when the money starts multiplying without you. Use your income to build a business. Once that business is stable, reinvest a portion of your profits into other businesses that will develop more cash flow. This should be a part of your retirement plan because when you can't work anymore you have to have money coming to sustain you.

COMMITMENTS FOR FINANCIAL CHANGE

- *I will not rely on others for my support.*
- *I will work to support myself, even if the job is not what I want.*
- *I will not let pride get in my way.*
- *I will exercise a good work ethic.*
- *I will be faithful on all of my job assignments.*
- *I will utilize my God given gifts/talents.*
- *I will accept opportunities to learn and grow even if it is an unpaid position.*
- *I will educate myself.*
- *I will create opportunities to learn.*
- *I will pursue fields that are in my passion.*
- *I will spend according to my income so I'm not forced to work multiple jobs.*
- *I will no longer work for money, but will let my money work for me.*
- *I will exercise good stewardship.*
- *I will teach my children stewardship principles.*

CHAPTER 9

Living on a Budget

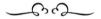

Once you have income coming in, you have to plan what you are going to do with it. Don't be a consumer who immediately spends it as soon as you earn it. Manage your money according to the level of income that you make. Our world system is going to offer you credit and opportunities to spend three times your income. Don't fall into that trap. You must continue to renew your mind in this area. You need to live below your means. If you're making $80,000.00 a year, you should live on $50,000.00 a year, because you need reserves. It is not advisable for you to live at the maximum of your income or above it.

In order for you to effectively eliminate debt you must have a budget. You need to control your spending, and restructure the amount of debt that you have. Remember to categorize your spending into needs versus wants as you evaluate your spending. If you don't currently use a budget you can use a daily spending log to help create one. A daily spending log requires you to write down everything you spend money on for a specific time period.

Once you log your activity, you'll be able to look at spending patterns. Some of them you may not be aware of, but once revealed they'll help you make changes. The spending log will be helpful in seeing where your money is going. From that point on, you'll think about where your money was spent when you balance your account. Most times when you use cash, you can't recall what it was spent on. But when you use debit cards they create a record and that helps you account for your spending.

A budget directs your income. A lot of people think a budget is restrictive, and it tells you what you can't do. In actuality the budget is you directing your money to where you think it will be most effective for you. You're making the decisions. If you're not happy with the budget you can modify it. You're the creator of the budget, and the controller of the budget. You can budget even if your income fluctuates because of commissions or other types of bonus income. If you have income that changes, decide how much you average each month. Always use your lowest averages and then project spending based on that number.

Among other things, your budget will include your housing, your utilities, and miscellaneous expenses. You'll also have a payment that represents the amount you'll have to pay to eliminate your debt. Your goal should be to balance the budget, make it more manageable, add things that are needed, delete things that are not, eliminate the debt and then increase your savings and reserves. Your daily spending log will help you identify what's going out and help you determine what adjustments need to be made. Some bills, like utilities, have a budget plan available through the company that keeps your bill at a fixed amount per month. If you can get them to set up a budget plan your budget won't change as much. You'll develop categories like schooling, for child expenses like activity fees, uniforms, and extra curricular activities. You want to put all of these expenses in your budget so that you know what has to go out every month. Finally, structure your budget so that there's money left over. There are going to be many unexpected expenses that you'll have to deal with.

Adhering to a budget may be initially challenging because you're going to have to go back and clean up some of the bad behavior that caused negative spending habits that led to the debt that you created. Your budget will help you make decisions like purchasing an affordable vehicle over an expensive one. Your budget will discipline and help you make changes to bring your finances in line. Your budget should help you leave a rental situation and purchase a home. You can make using a budget a fun tool in which you get your family involved. This will prevent your children from asking you to buy certain things. When you teach your children about setting goals, they will want to participate in the goals too. Your family finances will improve if you get the whole family to participate. As you work together, consider the following sample budget items:

- Rent/Mortgage
- Tithe/Giving
- Gas
- Electric
- Water
- Cable
- Telephone
- Food
- Miscellaneous
- Auto-Fuel
- Car Payment/Repairs
- Car insurance
- Debt payments
- Savings/Reserves
- Entertainment
- Personal Care
- Child Care
- Miscellaneous

COMMITMENTS FOR FINANCIAL CHANGE

- *I will live according to my income.*
- *I will exercise discipline.*
- *I will decrease my spending.*
- *I will live below my means.*
- *I will not spend just because I have money.*
- *I will manage my money using a budget.*
- *I will record and review my spending daily, weekly and monthly.*
- *I will use my budget to eliminate my debt.*
- *I will adjust my budget as needed.*
- *I will teach my children stewardship principles and include them in the family budget planning.*

CHAPTER 10

The Importance of Credit

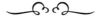

It is very important that you use credit wisely. One way to do this is to use your credit cards on thirty-day cycles. Using credit cards are good if you need to make a large purchase because it's not safe to travel with a lot of cash. Checks have so much of your information on them and have created problems like identity theft. If you have a charge on your credit card that's incorrect you can dispute it, but it's harder to get cash replaced into your bank account. So credit cards can be used for safety and for security.

There are things that you need to do that require a credit card. Some of these include purchasing an airplane ticket, renting a car, and traveling. In these situations it is beneficial to use credit cards. If you make purchases on credit, when the billing cycle ends you should pay the balance off. If you pay the balance in full at the end of the month you will avoid finance charges and additional fees. You should use all of your cards in that manner. An exception could be if you need to make a large purchase or if you have an unexpected major repair. You can use the credit card to spread the payment over a few months. This will subject you to some interest payments so get cards with the lowest rate. These are situations for homeowners that are unavoidable like having to replace a refrigerator, furnace, or hot water heater. Using reserves are better, but if there is no money in your reserve account then this is a time when it is beneficial to use credit.

Our spending habits have changed because credit is so readily available. Before credit cards were so readily available there were some alternatives. One alternative to credit was the layaway plan. Some stores still have layaway plans. It allowed people to do the same thing that we do now with the credit card in the reverse. Instead of making the purchase today and paying it over four months, you would lay everything away today, pay on it for four months, and then take it home. When layaway was a common option, people were not in debt like they are now. Now the credit card system allows you to buy everything today and then pay on it over time. So you buy more because credit allows you to purchase more than what you have money to buy. It's important that you stop making purchases that you don't have the money to pay for. Don't put things on credit cards that you can't pay immediately because the interest is the cost you pay for that convenience.

Once you get into the trap and you're charged interest, you pay more for the product than it cost.

Companies know that some accounts will be paid late and they will make additional money in late fees, over the limit fees, and other charges. Some of these charges are hidden in the fine print in your finance agreement. They hope that you won't manage your credit well so they can make more money from your account. Did you know that some credit cards offer you one rate and then raise it if you do not pay on time? You can miss making two payments and your interest rate can shift from 12 percent to 29 percent.

How many times have you felt like your bills were killing you? It's because debt is like death, and you have to free yourself from it. So if you are already in debt, you have to apply some debt elimination techniques to rid yourself of it. You may have as much as twenty to thirty thousand dollars worth of debt right now. You can't do anything about what you've already done in the past, but you can start fresh today. Develop a plan, analyze your situation, and cease all spending.

Your wants are subject to emotional spending. If you go to the store and purchase some clothing, don't take the tags off immediately. Take the tags off when you're going to wear it. Do you have things in your closet with tags on them? Why are you impulse buying? It's bad to buy on impulse, but when you buy on impulse and use credit that's worse! This lack of discipline causes unnecessary spending. Like I mentioned in chapter four, television is part of the problem. Advertising is designed to manipulate your thoughts to make you do something that you would not do. Have you ever said, "Why did I buy that"?

"Why did I do that?" It's because you were influenced. You have to limit the amount of influence that you allow yourself to be subjected to. Sometimes you have to put some discipline blocks in place. For example, pre-shop before shopping. Go look at the items in several stores and price compare them. If you still want to buy it, or you still need to buy it, you can make the purchase. If you don't have the money to buy it and it's a large appliance or similar item, then you can spread the payment over a three to four month period with the wise use of credit. If it's not something you need, then you shouldn't buy it, because you don't have the money.

I don't believe you should tear up all credit cards and never use them again. As mentioned earlier, I feel credit cards have benefits, like safety so that you're not walking around with a lot of cash. You need them when you travel. You may have to travel for your job, or you may need them for a vacation. You may have an emergency that requires credit. If you're purchasing things that are wants on a credit card, then you won't have spending privileges for your needs. You have to exercise self-discipline. When you make a charge to a credit account, then send the money in immediately. If you wait for the bill then finances charges will be included for every day since the purchase.

Have you ever said, "I work hard and I should treat myself"? If you don't have the money to treat yourself then you can't. It's as simple as that. You can't neglect a bill for a personal splurge. The phrase "I should pay myself first" was designed to talk about savings. When you are working, the IRS takes their deductions out of you income before you have access to it. When you receive your paycheck, the first thing you should after paying your tithes is take money out of your income and put it in a savings account. These reserves will protect you if your income is disrupted. Then you should pay your expenses and your budgeted debt obligations. The extra that's left over — your overflow — is to cover some of those wants within good reason.

Unfortunately, our world system is designed so that your credit has now become your integrity. A credit report doesn't always truly reflect the person, but to be honest more times than not it does. I think credit reports reflect your lack of financial education. It's not really an assessment of who you are as a person, but it really does show what you've been taught based on your behavior patterns. So much is based on credit, like jobs, housing, and insurance. You can't get utilities without a positive credit rating or you may have to pay a higher deposit to offset it. You can't purchase a home or rent an apartment, unless your credit has been analyzed. Your credit report is subject to errors, and needs to be monitored frequently, because it may not always be accurate. It can determine what interest rate you're going to be charged by a potential creditor. You need to understand what a credit report is, how to modify, change it, and make it better. Our financial system uses this report to determine your destiny and you must know what it is and how to understand it.

Your credit report is a report that lists the financial relationship that you've had with creditors over a period of time and what your performance was. For example, if you had a department store card, the credit report will show your balance owed and the required minimum payment per month. The report will also show if you paid as agreed, if you did not pay, or paid late. That report is going to have a rating system that's based on how many bills you have, your payment history, and your balances. When merged together, all of these different scenarios form your score. You're rated based on your credit score, so you need to know how it affects you, and learn how to work within its guidelines to earn a successful rating. That report may not reflect who you are, so you need to learn to conquer the system.

It is prudent for you to see your credit report every six months to a year to see what's on it. Identity theft and fraud are on the rise in our marketplace, so you want to make sure that your report is accurate. Creditors are going to use it to judge you and make decisions about you. Once you assess its accuracy, some of the things that are on it may need to be improved. It should reflect your current spending patterns and not the financial mistakes that you used to make.

There may be an entry on the report that is incorrect. Unfortunately these negative reports affect your score, and that score affects things that you may be trying to do. You can correct items on the credit report that are wrong. It takes a lot of effort and persistence. You do not want a false report to delay your goals.

You have to monitor your report, and make corrections as needed.

You may have to call the creditor, write letters and show receipts. Organize your life like it's a business. Keep records, and copies of correspondence, because you may need these for proof. During the investigation keep a notebook of the people you speak to and record the dates of the conversations. These records are going to be very critical. You don't want to be held up when you are at that point of breakthrough. You may need to get your records in order to get something resolved.

You may find yourself in a situation where a creditor didn't have the right address information and you never received a bill. The report may show that you are someone who doesn't pay when in reality that's not what happened. You have to defend your rights and be persistent until it is corrected.

You have to fight for what is right. You have to prove that you didn't do some things. You have to fight for records to be changed. There are people with similar or the same names whose credit files may be merged together. If your children are named after you, then your credit reports may not distinguish the "senior" from the "junior." Also when you have twins, and they have the exact same initials, birth date, and address, the credit bureau may not tell them apart. Common names often cause problems.

Thus far in your reading, you should have learned that you must understand our world system and your relationship with income, how to manage your money with a budget, the importance of stewardship principles, how to stay out of debt, and how to use your credit report to your advantage.

COMMITMENTS FOR FINANCIAL CHANGE

- *I will limit my spending.*
- *I will spend my money on needs and not wants.*
- *I will limit my wants and purchase them out of overflow.*
- *I will manage my credit wisely.*
- *I will protect my self against identity theft.*
- *I will pay all my credit cards within the thirty-day billing period.*
- *I will review my credit reports every six months to a year.*
- *I will keep sufficient reserves.*

CHAPTER 11

Vision Planning

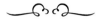

It is very important that you have a vision plan for your life. Proverbs 21:5 states that "The plans of the diligent lead surely to plenty, but those of everyone who is hasty, surely to poverty." What is your vision plan? Have you written one? It can incorporate a business plan, personal improvement, goals, desires and dreams. All of your focus and energy needs to be on your vision plan. Once you write it, you have to pursue it as aggressively as you can. You have to be intensely focused on the vision and concentrate on it so it will come to pass. Don't be distracted. Write the plan and don't allow other things to pull your focus in other directions. Once you write the plan, break that plan down into timelines and tasks that you can accomplish in the interim. Chip away at it by doing something towards the plan each day, each week, each month, each year, then ultimately the complete vision will come to pass. This is because each day you made an effort to fulfill that plan.

Focus on the end result. Focus on the time frame that you have to apply yourself. Keep the plan to daily, weekly, and monthly assignments so you can meet your goal. Use the available time that you have so that every day, every week, you are doing something that keeps you on track with the timeline and gets you closer to your goal.

How can you take some of these ideas to fundamental application? After you break your vision plan down into smaller tasks, make sure that you are touching every aspect of the plan everyday. If you have a goal to become physically fit, lose weight, and eat healthier, then each day you have to evaluate the meals that you intake. Each day you evaluate your schedule to make sure that there is time for you to exercise.

Another example is furthering your education. Determine how long it will take based on the time that you can spend, in order for you to receive the next degree level. Then take the specific amount of classes and credit hours each semester, in order to fulfill those requirements in the time frame that you want.

If you find that the program requires twelve semester hours and you have a responsibility to your family, your children, and your church, then evaluate how much time you can dedicate to school. If you can take, six semester hours, then it will take two semesters to reach the twelve semester hours required. If the semester lasts half a year that you're a year away from applying for that job. So what's next? Go ahead and register knowing that in a year you will have the credentials you want. Stay on that path until you accomplish that. If something happens, then make some adjustments, change the plan, and keep going.

A vision plan goal could be to own a home. People who own their own home usually live in better neighborhoods. These neighborhoods usually have better schools. There are tax benefits to owning a home. Wealth is generated from building equity in the home from principal reduction and appreciation. Your first step would be to speak with a mortgage lender. If you have debt that has to be paid off, set timelines on how long it would take to do this. If you were advised to increase your income in order for you to qualify for your loan then that would tie into an employment or job change. There could be so many components of trying to get a home. If you need to increase your income, then start looking for other opportunities for promotion. Find out whatever is required and then start working on it.

You may need to make some modifications in your spending to accumulate the down payment. With that one change, you could be sitting in front of your fireplace, in a year enjoying the Christmas season with your family in your new home.

In many aspects of your life, you exercise the components of a vision plan but never formally structure it. This causes those goals to get delayed. The plan helps you track your progress, which helps you reach those goals quicker.

It's very important that you stay focused. It's very important that you remain committed. It is very important that you don't give up and that you encourage yourself. You may not have people in your life to encourage you so you have to know how to encourage yourself. What motivates you? Use whatever motivates you to move forward. If it's writing notes to yourself, posting pictures of goals, or just having some quiet time, then do it. Find the source of your goal.

If your goal is to be retired, then visualize yourself there. In your quiet time, imagine being in that place where your goal is realized. Can you imagine waking up early in the morning with a plan to advance the Kingdom of God? When you imagine yourself at the point where your goal is realized then you'll get there quicker. Continue to motivate yourself by imagining yourself in that place.

Some people have all the information and don't do anything with it. Some of them are afraid. I've tried before and I failed. If you talk to a lot of people who are successful and those who are wealthy – you'll find a common thread. They tried and they failed. You have to eliminate the fear of failure.

I don't avoid failure anymore. Failure is a part of my growth, development and success. Failure is a part of the wealth building process. When I made financial mistakes, I examined my critical errors. At first it really bothered me and I started to feel like a failure. Quickly I realized that the experience was good for me. It gave me the opportunity to make some corrections, and change some of my behaviors so that I wouldn't be in the same situation again. When I find that I am operating in error, I make corrections in order to improve my situation. When executing your vision plan, allow for mistakes.

My vision plan included writing this book. I had to structure my day, and effectively manage my time. Everyday I spent 1-2 hours on the book to make sure it moved forward. When I did not have a structured time for it, three years went by and the book hadn't made any progress.

Consider this example. If you have a job and you are running a business on the side, how can you make a transition to running your business full time? How do you exit your full-time job and then get into that place where you want to be? Identify what you want to do. Do your research to find out if you need to take classes, or apply for licenses. Make that list. Do the tasks. Get the necessary credentials to make the necessary changes.

If you want to transition into a new job, or start a business, you have to look at your schedule. You have to look at your day and use time that you are spending on television or other important things, and redirect that time to your goal. If you want to transition from one job into another one you have to budget your schedule. If your heart isn't in what you do and your job isn't where you're supposed to be, sacrifice to make the change.

If you feel like there's not enough time in the day, exercise time management skills to maximize your day. Take better care of yourself so you will have more energy. Fill your mind with positive things and surround yourself with people who encourage and help you. Keep working hard because the vision plan that you execute today will be the reality that you will live tomorrow.

COMMITMENTS FOR FINANCIAL CHANGE

- *I will write a vision plan.*
- *I will review my plan regularly.*
- *I will modify my plan as needed.*
- *I will stay focused.*
- *I will encourage myself.*
- *I will pursue my goals.*

CHAPTER 12

Pursuing Your Dreams

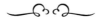

In order to move forward, decide what you want for your life. You are in control. Evaluate your plan and identify your destiny position. If you aren't sure what it is, then first discover your gifts, talents, and your passion, by taking a look within yourself.

Who are you? Why are you here? What is your purpose? Why does God have you here? What are your talents? As your mind is renewed, you will discover who you are in Christ. Once you answer these critical questions then you can achieve your dreams. You will have hope, because you have purpose. You'll no longer feel like a hamster in a cage just going around on a never-ending wheel.

God has something for you. Get your resources in place so that you can break into other areas in your life. There are many great opportunities that will satisfy you. This will help you accomplish something that benefits you. After you master this, prepare to teach your children so the knowledge will pass from generation to generation. This way you will be able to be a vessel of hope. You will help them be productive, find their purpose, and know who they are. This way they will not be sidetracked into unproductive cycles.

Don't get discouraged if something happens and you have to modify the timeline. Just do it, stay encouraged, stay on the path, and keep your faith. Surround yourself with people who have similar goals. Get some people to be your cheerleaders. Find people who are in your corner and who are going to continue to root you on. You are going to have friends that can walk with you because you will have similar goals. You can do some joint projects together. You will also have some friends whose goals are totally different than yours. You can pray for them, encourage them, and be a supportive friend to them.

With your renewed mind and new way of thinking, evaluate your willingness to go the distance. There are things that you may have to overcome. It can be a very difficult process, and this is why everyone is not wealthy. Each time you are faced with challenges you have a few choices. You can give up, you can accept your life as it is, or you can settle because you are better off than most people. However, if you're really willing, you can make the sacrifices that it takes to change your situation. Wouldn't it be good to arrive at that point in your life where you want to be? With sacrifices and hard work it's possible. With God, all things are possible.

If you attended college you are familiar with staying up all night to get an assignment completed. You have a lot of energy when you are in college so you can cram all night for your exams, and survive on two hour's sleep. You pushed yourself when you had a paper due or another assignment to turn in. Caffeine was used as a tool to get you through the night and you would get it done. Once you passed the exam you completed the class. That brought you closer to your goal of a college degree. Are you committed daily to work toward your goals like those working for a college degree? You may not have that same youthful energy, but are you willing to cram all night for your success? Are you willing to stay up all night to finish a proposal that's due the next day? What if you had an opportunity to present an idea to a prospective investor? Would that be worth the sacrifice? How willing are you?

You have to be more committed to your success than anyone else. I had a friend who was interested in breaking into the lending field. I was in the Real Estate business and made many contacts over the years. I spoke to a manager about interviewing him and because of our relationship he said he would do it the next day. I gave my friend the telephone number, the manager's name, and told him to call to set up the interview, but he never called. This was a unique opportunity where my friend was able to bypass the entire pre-employment process, and be granted an immediate interview. All he had to do was call the manager for an appointment, but he never did.

When you decide that you want something, other people will go the distance to help you get it. They may do work for you and make the opportunity available. Are you willing to follow through? Is someone else going to work harder for you than you will for yourself? So think about your goals because when people open doors for you, favor is granted. God's favor allows you to bypass some of the harder challenges that you would normally have to go through. When you throw it away, you send a message to the person who helped you that you are a bad investment. You are telling them not to invest in you again, because you are going to waste their time.

I've found that a lot of people talk in their peer circles. It's popular to talk about success and what you are going to do, who you are going to be, and where you are going to go. But many of these people talk about things they never do. How many follow through and make sure that these things happen? How willing are you to make it happen? Do you talk big in your peer group to impress them? What do you want to do? If someone's giving you information that you can use to reach your goal, apply yourself and make it happen.

One day you will arrive at the point that you worked and prayed for. The gifts and talents that were put in you will manifest and you will reach your destiny position. It was your acceptance of the gift in you, your willingness to work hard and persevere, and your patience that got you to the day that your dream becomes a reality. Everybody wants the wealth, to get rich quick, without having to work.

Wealth requires life changes, taking chances, and sacrifice. It is a very difficult process.

There are so many types of process. Most people don't understand the value of "process" so they want to bypass it. When I lived in New York City, we had trains that stopped at every station. These trains were called the local. There were some trains that used some middle tracts and they would just go right by. These were called the express. At certain train stops, and you could get on the local, or you could get on the express. In life everybody wants the express. We want to bypass all the small stops along the way and just get straight to the destination. Some of those smaller stops have lessons and experiences that make you stronger for the destination that you are heading toward. When you bypass process, you miss lessons along the way. Sometimes you miss the appreciation of the arrival at the final destination, because you got there too quick. Sometimes that process allows you to appreciate how hard you worked for something, so that when you get to the end, you will fight for it.

I've seen people purchase homes with no down payment. They didn't have anything vested in it, so when they lost the house in foreclosure they said, "It's no big deal. I didn't pay anything for it".

You are going to have times that you decide a direction for your life, then life changes. When life changes, you may have to change the path that you thought you were going to take. The wonderful part of life is that you get to decide. The plan that you had two years ago is no longer the plan now. When you shift gears and you go in a new direction, you have to let go of that old plan and pursue the new one. You have to be flexible, and you have to be willing to accept change. I've seen people purchase a property that was perfect for them. It was their dream house, but then their elderly parent came to live with them. This was not expected, and the house was not conducive to the elderly parent living there. So they had to sell the house. They thought it was their dream house and that they would live there forever. Now they live in something that is more conducive for the whole family.

Life's events may alter your vision plan. Does that mean that the vision plan was incorrect? No that's just how life is. It's just like your budget. You get to control your budget and modify it so that it fits your agenda. Just remember that you're in control so when challenges occur and things don't go as planned, you can take the helm from the driver's seat. Don't be afraid, because when you start moving towards your goal, fear increases. The fear will get stronger as you get closer to the prize. Just remember that. When you're almost there the fear is astronomical, and the challenges will increase. The bumps in the road get harder. If you turn around too soon, you may miss your victory around the corner.

As you deal with these challenges and as you deal with life, you'll be the trailblazer. You're the person that gets to go where no one has gone before. You won't always have a reference. I'm one of those people. I didn't have the people to call who did the business that I did, or did it the way that I did, to ask questions. Because I didn't know people who had started a business like I did, I had to learn the hard way. Now I'm one of the people that other people can come to and ask their questions so that they won't experience the bumps that I did. Sometimes we get fearful because it hurts to fall, and we can build defense mechanisms that will stop us from falling again. If you fall a couple of times, when you get up the prize is greater.

Combat the fear with this prayer:

"Lord I know you have called me to do great things and I accept the call. Lord I can't operate in my own strength because my flesh wants to give up. Lord I need to move in your strength. Give me wisdom and empower me. Make provision for your work to come to pass through me. Lord my spirit may get discouraged but you sent your comforter the Holy Spirit to guide me through this. Lord I know fear is not of you, because you have not given us the spirit of fear. Take these emotions away that I may stay focused on the task at hand. Amen."

Surround yourself with your support group that you formed to cheer you on. Continue to fight the fear so you will go forward. You are closer. Every time I looked back to where I came from, I chose to go forward. I just kept moving, even if a little fear was on me. I think fear is an indication that you're doing the right thing. Fear encompasses change. Change means that life is about to be different, you have to take some risk, you have to be uncomfortable, and you have to get out of your comfort zone. Wealthy people do not remain in their comfort zone. You have to come out the box and do some different things. If you're doing what everybody else is doing then you are a part of the masses of people who live an average life. It's when you come out the box, get ridiculed, and have people talk about you that you make it. They will call you crazy! Your circle of friends will get smaller and you won't have as many supporters. This is because you're doing something radical that no one's seen before. So stay encouraged and don't let that stop you.

COMMITMENTS FOR FINANCIAL CHANGE

- *I will succeed!*

Printed in the United States
125648LV00001B/1/P

9 781606 473900